Hunger In A Cat's Yellow Eye

POEMS

Hunger In A Cat's Yellow Eye

POEMS

by
William Snyder Jr.

Encircle Publications, LLC
Farmington, Maine USA

Hunger In A Cat's Yellow Eye ©2020 William Snyder Jr.

Paperback ISBN-13: 978-1-64599-123-6
e-Book ISBN-13: 978-1-64599-124-3
Kindle ISBN-13: 978-1-64599-125-0

All rights reserved. No part of this book may be reproduced in any form by any mechanical or electronic means including storage and retrieval systems without express written permission in writing from the publisher. Brief passages may be quoted in review. Rights to individual poems and essays remain with authors.

Editor: Cynthia Brackett-Vincent
Book and book cover design: Eddie Vincent/ENC Graphics Services
Cover Image: Shutterstock.com

Sign up for Encircle Publications newsletter and specials
http://eepurl.com/cs8taP

Printing: Walch Publishing, Portland, Maine

Mail Orders, Author Inquiries:
Encircle Publications
PO Box 187
Farmington, ME USA 04938
207-778-0467

Online orders:
encirclepub.com

ACKNOWLEDGEMENTS

Apalachee Quarterly: "Hunger in a Cat's Yellow Eye"
California Quarterly: "River Crossing"
Caveat Lector: "A Crown of Jokes"
Chaffin Journal: "A Train into Morning"
Connecticut River Review: "Inventions"
The Cresset: "On the Bending of Light"
Descant: "A Journey of Climbing"
El Portal: "June Eight Park"
Habersham Review: "In a Round World of Come and Go"
The Helix: "Company"
Kestrel: "A World of Understanding" and "The Dry Heat of Afternoons"
The Long Islander: "Love Suffers Here"
Louisiana Literature: "What Happens to Color"
The MacGuffin: "A Certainty of Heat"
Mankato Poetry Review: "Weights"
National Forum: "And Leaving after Time"
Santa Fe Literary Review: "What I Get I Deserve"
Weber Studies: "Grace" and "To Speak of Leaving"
Wind Magazine: "There Forever"
Worcester Review: "The Trains Run Irregularly"

To
Wendy Bishop (1953–2003), Florida State University
(Kellogg W. Hunt professor of English, 2000–2003)

Table of Contents

Acknowledgements

Love Suffers Here 1
The Trains Run Irregularly 2
On the Bending of Light 3
A Journey of Climbing 4
In a Round World of Come and Go 5
Hunger in a Cat's Yellow Eye 6
The Dry Heat of Afternoons 7
Grace 8
River Crossing 10
Weights 11
A World of Understanding 12
Inventions 13
A Train into Morning 15
What Happens to Color 16
A Certainty of Heat 17
A Crown of Jokes 18
June Eight Park 19
Company 20
What I Get I Deserve 22
And Leaving after Time 23
To Speak of Leaving 24
There Forever 26

About the Author 27

LOVE SUFFERS HERE

The bare lamp by our bedside works shadows,
but choices are possible, even in this light.
I follow your gaze to a middle distance
up the hills—the red, sloping roofs,
white clothes flapping, strung above
the tiny plots walled in white, and narrow steps
planing up to so much blue. But islands
suit us better, I say, are better suited
to days like these—what people mean
when they say that everyone does survive.
And too, there are tiny bars. And bungalows
by the rocks where women serve cabbage soup
and leek. But here, the sun strikes crescents
on small, white windows. School children
singsong on the street beneath our room.
The tune you hum is nameless,
your brown eyes absorbing everything.

THE TRAINS RUN IRREGULARLY

We board the local back to the city.
Wheel-clicks accelerate. The old coaches—
sides of slatted wood, netted racks
above the open windows—trundle over
sagging track. Two stops in, hard
in the wooden seats, we run
to the baggage van. The train
grumbles on. You stand, weight
on one foot, hands on the bar
across the door-space, and the sun,
as we curve south, flames your fingers
and delicate webs. This is how I know you
now—silhouette against an orange world.
We jostle through the yard
past wagons, splaying rails,
workers in blue smoking cigarettes.
I hold my lips to your cheek's sharp bone.

ON THE BENDING OF LIGHT

It is almost quiet. A woman calls—faint, unperturbed—
for her child perhaps, her husband. A clock
in the room below strikes three. Now the answering
bells outside. And even as a moped
loots us raw, we feel a sense of luxury.
This is not luxury—but it is enough—this room,
the narrow window open to the street, the pale,
moiré curtains shifting in and out, and the light—
shaping, reshaping the wooden drawers,
the tiny white basin, the faded blue tiles. And our skin—
toes to lips. On these thin sheets, we return
to ourselves, searching hands and mouths
for the softest textures of memory—and to acknowledge
the luxury of things. And the almost quiet.

A JOURNEY OF CLIMBING

Alone, I climb the Hill of Steps, this steep
climb above the harbor
where tourists once lingered.
I imagine them paused on promontories,
leaning against the low, stone walls—the subjects
of photographs. The stairs are cracked now,
stones old and yellow. Weeds grow
from earth showing through.

The harbor flashes chrome
as light shifts west. I climb past houses
poised on terraces, staggered
one above another. A flock of stiff, white garments
flaps above a parcel of grass. A workman
on a ladder drags a fat brush of white
across a wall, his companion
scraping shards of old paint below.

In a house by the steps, its roof spouts
fanning orange down its foundation, a woman
in white—taffeta, or cotton—stares
at her fingers on a round, glass table
at which she sits. I watch, sensing she will not
look up. She knows this hill.

IN A ROUND WORLD OF COME AND GO

We ring. The door opens, and a man—slack brown suit,
black hair, comb-lines above his ears. Hello, he says,
yes, I have a room, a room for the night,
and he leads us down the hall in blue light, blue glass
above the door. To the dining room and wooden tables,
white cloth, a fireplace mantle with a row of cups.

Yes, he says, he will serve us breakfast tomorrow,
himself. Do we like his collection, his cups? Are they
intriguing? Yes, we say, and he says yes,
they are very valuable, come to me many years ago
from the grandmother, yes, now dead, sorry to say,
in the war, dead, but her cups, I like them here.

On one, blue enamel, the rim a smooth, round ring.
Simple. And white inside, like teeth, an inner thigh,
and outside, gold leaf that frames a sky
of churning gray clouds—a world inside this cup.
And before these clouds a cherub with one faint red,
blue, and yellow wing. She rests behind a pillow,
chin cupped in hollow palm, staring up
to the dark wood wainscot, ignoring our gazes.

Yes, cobalt, the man says, a beautiful shade, a blue,
the blue of blue. And he asks our needs
for breakfast and we say simple, and he is pleased,
and smiles, shakes our hands. These cups, he says, simple,
like your breakfast will be, yes, but we will
not use these cups tomorrow.

HUNGER IN A CAT'S YELLOW EYE

You want the Christ with the most wounds,
so we cross to the old quarter—the little shops
of statues and thorns. On a street, men haul
octopus, tentacles stiff in ice. Fat gulls
swoop above. I cup your neck, search my fingers
up your skull. You turn. And your eyes—
pupils tiny and black
in a gray-webbed blue, your lids
halfway. In a window, a huge cat,
its one glassy eye reflecting everything:
yellow clouds wrap a now-green sky,
and the two of us, like faces
in an old, spooling print, or a playbill—
not quite you, not quite me—but skewed,
out of round. I search inside the eye,
and only there. Because I cannot turn, one simple
turn to face you, to say, I need. A bell jingles.
A man comes out, loops
across the eye and over clouds. My face remains—
smooth, yellow, glass. A bicycle clinks,
water runs the gutter from a fish house hose,
Christs ooze in every window. You call
from next door. Forty-one, you say, forty-one.

THE DRY HEAT OF AFTERNOONS

A fishing boat, prow inlaid with gulls,
cuts the harbor to the dock, hands
on board gathering seines. Punts bobble
nearby. A man tugs a rope
hand over hand and a pot emerges,
shimmering black, inside, a maze
of tentacles. A ship lists in shadows.
Sprays of light rustle eddies and swirls.
Fish leap. Ripples swirl the calm,
as ships disturb the calms around them.

It is not time to stay here. We know this.
The rooms near the station
are full. The post office is closed.
The changers refuse our notes.
It is like a movie. Like a picture on a card.

GRACE

We wake to the late afternoon—August heat,
street-side chatter, smells of charcoal
and grilling fish. We wander out, groggy, hungry.
But down a street, music, and we follow it,
and find a stage on a square where two men
play accordions, a woman a clarinet. An old man
dances, claps his hands and people laugh, whistle,
urge him on. The band plays a waltz,

and children in white and blue, jingles sewn
to collars and sleeves, do a local step—turns
and dips. One girl, short hair, forehead
glistened with sweat, dances with them, her lips
just-drawn at the corners to a smile. This smile—
and her eyes—dark, almond-round, skin calm
and new around them—speak a knowingness
of fingertips, of calves and thighs, muscles

shaping gesture and skin. Her arms rise,
snap across her chest to pull a spin
and she whirls. She faces us, feet skipping
right-toe-stamp, and she sees us, she must—
in knots and stands on the cobblestones—
how we watch, how we have to watch, as we would
a fire, a field of phlox. And all the dancers,
holding hands, swoop and spin. And the music ends.

The dancers bow, step down. The girl hugs the man
who danced—her grandfather perhaps, and I
imagine, deep inside of her, between her lips
and heart, a basin filled with dance, with joy,
with what it is to be this girl, with what it is

to know of grace. Now we hunt a café for beer,
bread, peppery fish. I demonstrate my dancing. Kick-
jump-stumble. You laugh, push me aside.

RIVER CROSSING

The skiff slides toward us.
A man in thick, brown corduroy
works the pole. Ripples surge,
ease, rush from the keel. We will
climb in, sit on the lacquered bench.

The man will point the skiff
upstream, and with his pole,
and with the drift, will find
the place across. His wife,
waiting for him there, will splash

through the shallows
and steady the skiff, and the man
will carry us, one at a time,
to the bank on his back.
He will not be embarrassed.

WEIGHTS

On this seawall, my arms in my hands,
I feel adrift. The sea curves far away. I feel
the melancholy press of waves and salt,
of late afternoons alone. Beyond
the seaweed man, with his basket and rake,
they work—leaping, splashing—boys
in single file dragging long, slender nets into
the surf. The lead boys jump swells, bob,
swim out to surround the fish. Three old men
call and cajole from the sand, gesturing
sparrow bones and sagging skin. The boys
ignore these men and draw
their nets as always. The looping circle closes,
and when feet touch bottom the boys
shake heads, spew water, spray
hazy ribbons through the dark red sun.
They lean now, their backs to the waves,
pulling toward the foam-spliced shallows
and the old men. And toward the wall.
Toward me. Distance and years
are impossible to gauge—like these boys,
a catch of fish, tides, a whisper.

A WORLD OF UNDERSTANDING

You pause on the cathedral step, yellow hat
above your eyes, your summer dress
airy blue, airy flutter. An old woman
sits by the wooden doors, holds a paper cup.
You shake your head, step higher, brown shoes
clicking marble. Below, with
their wooden carts of saints, candles, beads,
trinket dealers fiddle change.

In the café last night, over bottles, empty
and green, men stared at you. I felt
the strum of anger, white-edged—opened flesh
before the blood—at your yellow hat,
your arms, their strength a wonder
each time you hold me, and at your resistance,
even as you hold me.

In the nave, candle smoke sours eyes. The cream-
skinned statues, blood pinching out
from wounds, might quicken us
to understanding, blood a purchase for pleasure.
But all this suffering. Did they cry out? Slump
into bitterness? Must it always cost so?

Then back to our room—our rug shaken, bed
straightened by the woman
who saves our room for last, as if
she loathes our stories in towel and sheet.
Showers will blow through toward morning,
gray rain, off and on. It is not the suffering
that angers the most.

INVENTIONS

1

The days please us—the sun, the speckled sea
as we climb the steps above the town,
the little blue flowers
squeezing up from chinks and cracks. Nights
we chronicle with our tiers
of thigh, hip, chest, smoothings
of fingertips like shamans might, nuzzles
into shallows and folds.

2

One morning, with the sun shaping
curtain patterns, we discover writing—
pencil scrawls on the headboard wall.
We puzzle these letters-lines into tableau:
a prisoner, escaped, reckoning time;
a traveler, money lost by docks
or indiscretion, scribbling herself home;
lovers scheming finer ways to love
in a world so cornered against them.

3

A freighter, long-rusted, lists
in the pier-side shallows. To be in
its shadow, to feel the pressures of current
on leaky plates, to hear
the gulls wheel about a woman tossing
crusts from her dark blue apron, is to know
we will never know the sure. So we retrace,

veer back to the true: bed sheet and blanket,
hip-crease and damp, little blue flowers
on thread-blown stems.

A TRAIN INTO MORNING

The hint of grit on cushions and curtains.
The scraping of steel. And through the dark windows,
into night-space, tiny lights appear, disappear, like voices
left on platforms. Your night-weight
against my shoulder, you sleep, dream, or you
stay awake, thinking—the train too loud
for me to know. This morning, I turned to you
across the bed, felt you shift, felt you change
(felt that you had changed), that somewhere
deep inside of you (or me) a burr had blossomed
on the cord connecting us. Do you think, or dream
that I have given up, or lost some part of me
that once was warm, and because of that,
the burr began to swell, will one day split wide,
exposing inner flesh? Tomorrow, we'll decide again.
But I will not be able to ask you about the burr,
because tonight, on this train, you seem
so usual—your ankles crossed, fingers laced. I
dream the ordinary most—deep, unknowable.
I dream that words between us, when we speak,
might polish that burr, buff it almost smooth,
almost gone, like water might granite or quartz—
almost never there. The train jolts through sidetrack
switches, sways through joints. Crossing bells
clamber. These rails were dreams once too.

WHAT HAPPENS TO COLOR

A skiff lies keel down on the riverbank.
Up the yard, a cottage—egg blue walls,
brown shutters. And lantana, pruned
to squares, globes, a candelabra even,
bloom in circle plots. An old woman
in a blue smock carves away
some blooms. Downstream, the city
blooms white—the hillside steps,
cathedral candles, sheets, and with
the sun, the sea glows white
in early afternoon. And now this cottage,
and the green river, and the lantana's
rings of yellow bells and pink.
White could disappear, turn clear,
transparent like a cornea cup, and hard
to touch. The woman steps from her stool,
nods. Her skin is dark, her eyes brown.
I would ask her about color, and the urge
to shape, but embarrassed—to be
standing here, and without the words
to speak—I wave, walk on, beyond
a poplar wall, farther still from the city.

A CERTAINTY OF HEAT

Two men talk on the square—foot-shuffle, finger-point.
Another sweeps the cobblestones, his shirt-back
dark with sweat. Water sips from the fountain
behind them, pools in cracks, catches light.
You roll your glass along your cheek, up your arm,
your skin gathering moisture like people do lips or scent.
You say you will dip your feet in the fountain,
fan your hair, wring water down your back.

But the people, I say. They would too, you say,
but they haven't time, or they're used to it.
The cathedral stands open, a row of candles
just inside. A woman curls on the steps. If sunlight
could flicker dark it would now, and pull us up
to a cold unburdening. Draw us down through stone.
A horse cart stops on the street, pitchforks loose
on the dusty cart-bed. A man beside us
calls to the driver, waves him to move, but the driver

stares ahead—beyond the steeple glowing bronze,
beyond the egg-white haze, the silver air. Urine,
sweat, the steeple, the square in the rush of a long day.
You push from the table. It's too hot, you say,
you will fold your dress. It is a white dress,
with blue designs like Delft. You walk behind the cart,
ankles tipping with the offset stones. I feel
the hush, the men at the tables holding your walk.
Your shoulders and hair. White and blue and wet.

A CROWN OF JOKES

A butcher's window frames a slick, white head on ice. The calf's blue-black eyes stare up through shadows to the cupolas across the street, or to the sky. I've been morose, you tell me. My behavior at the café last night embarrassed you when the men bought us rounds, toasting our fertility.

So today, I try to act funny, though I can count my jokes on one finger. I do see them, jokes, like the Christs in the shops by the cathedral: sinewy bodies punctured, nailed, oozing blood from puckered wounds. Today is a failure. Punch lines elude me. Drum rolls elude me. But I was funny once, I say. Honest. No kidding.

This Calf's head and Crucifix wait patiently before the Pearly Gates. Calf's head turns to crucifix, says, Saint Peter's screening for hang-ups today, what's yours? Or. This scrawny guy, lugging a two-ton log, stuck by thirty-two arrows, nine hundred and six acacia thorns, stumbles into a saloon. The bartender asks, what'll it be? The guy sighs, looks to the ceiling, says, gimme a Rusty Nail.

Or. There's a man and a woman in this old city, in a shop, ringed by pasty figures and grisly weapons. The woman is vexed. With a string of jokes, the man tries to temper her dark mood, his own uneasiness. But the woman will not smile. Nor do the Christs. A dead audience, the man complains. Or.

JUNE EIGHT PARK

Snapdragons and periwinkle bloom
in weed-choked beds. I know
these flowers. And weeds. But not
birds. These small birds
with yellow crests making
flutter-baths in pools of dust.
In a café nearby, photographs
of men carving topiary in this park—
ostrich, giraffe, turtle—now
grown wild. People stroll here—
children, men in jackets with
wide, blotter ties. Old women
nestle in on bench-ends. Random things,
how they settle or pass, and
the confusion of voices tilt me
out of plumb. I want those words,
those animal trees, those birds, as all
these people here must know them.

COMPANY

The café door open to the street,
the seven tables occupied tonight, one
by troopers in uniform. A bony cat
slinks through chair legs and rungs.
We listen to the calms and quicks
of conversations until the owners,
two brothers, bring our food—fresh prawn,
onion, butter, bread. Suddenly, the cat
leaps to our table. I brush it off
and the owners chase it, apologize, pat
our shoulders, bring fresh wine.
The troopers laugh, pound backs. One
pings his glass with a fork.

The cat creeps back. A trooper tempts
it with coos and a knife, its blade
spearing shells. The cat leaps toward
the dangle. The trooper raises the knife.
The cat eyes the shells, springs again—four,
five, six times—claws spread, ears
erect, but the knife is jerked up
just far enough. Someone behind us
makes a hiss. The owners polish trays
at the kitchen door. Another leap.
The trooper darts his hand, throws
the cat and it tumbles. Another hiss.
A whistle. The cat leaps, fur-lines taut.
The trooper slashes downward, but the cat
twists, the blade flashing past.

The cat licks its flank. The trooper
drops the knife—blade first—but the cat
springs aside. We hoot for the cat, clap.

The trooper smiles, leans back, thrusts his legs—
accepts our applause. A woman glowers,
reaches toward the cat. Tail quivering, it licks
the bread, the juice and prawn she's offered.

WHAT I GET I DESERVE

We find ourselves by the river.
The far side is stone—
customs house, the city gate—
our side grassy with a gravel walk.
We are alone. There is no moon.
A street lamp sends dim shadows
to us, to the river—a gurgle
of black and silver swirling
past the bulwark stones.
I find mucus deep in my throat,
and though you hate this,
form an O with my lips
and blow, toss it
far onto the water where it bobs,
a shining dot running down. I wager
tomorrow, and tonight you're game.
You search deep and toss.
But saliva sprays
and dribbles down your chin
and we burst
with laughter. It is women's
singular failing, I say. You agree,
then remind me of my own.

AND LEAVING AFTER TIME

Our train curved in to the station. We'll stop
for a day, we said, a few days—the cathedral
is famous, the octopus men are
something to see. We stayed near the park,
undecided, train schedule ready. Days passed—
we'll go to this café or that café, we said.
We'll walk the hillside steps once more.
We'll visit the sea again. And again.
The schedule crumpled. Creases tore. Then
went lost—beneath a bench, behind
a bed, on a table after wine. The days
became *where for coffee? At two or three?*
When to eat? Early or late? What to do?
What to do? Days passed. And with purpose
sometimes, ennui sometimes, we began
to push within: *I'll go alone. You spend*
too much time. I think you. You seem to—
until yesterday and the red roofs,
the octopus urns stacked lip to lip, the sun—
its long, shimmering line down the sea.
All this so easy again. And today, the timetable
at the ticket window easy to understand,
coach-steps easy to climb.

In that room near the park, the window
open for light, a woman
leans her mop, opens drawers for a sock
or change, finds a tattered schedule—time-rows
and columns down come true at last.

TO SPEAK OF LEAVING

The mottled pier—hard stones mortared over
long ago. A wooden boat sways
in the calm below. Eddies gurgle farther out,
and farther still, currents and the sun
weave fissures and whirls.

The ferry arrives. Men hold hawsers as we board.
There is no need to cry. The reasons for anything
are exaggerated here, and recognized easily,
like the ferry's name in red
around the life preservers; the cuckoos
beyond the rough, stone walls inland (just last hour);
and the little store—bins of tiny, sea-salt potatoes
hand-dug from loam.

It would be nothing
to be flung away to an untethered somewhere—
floating, desirable. The engines vibrate. Exhaust throbs
upward. I lie on a wooden bench, watch the sky,
the low clouds scooting against us. You join me.
Too noisy below. Say something.

Say the wish to stay, though now, too late.
The wish to stay alone. Too late.
What do we want—longing
confused with desire? Touch is important
no longer. That is the feeling now, my feeling (yours?)
though we touch, for a moment as the ferry plunges
down a green wave and up another—we touch—

shoulders and arms through cotton and wool,
through skin, warm skin, but colder now
than in our narrow bed (just this morning) three,

four blankets thick, piled on against the rain,
the fog. Say something. It is clearer now,
here, the sun even—and that's what makes it hard.

THERE FOREVER

We stand in the heart of here—bus station,
square of walks and trees, statues
of men on horseback. A photo-for-hire man
adjusts his camera—black box, black cloth shroud
like vaudeville or circa print. The man,
in white shirt and narrow black tie is happy
for our coins. We are in his world—his lens,

his mirror and glass. And out again
to light, to us, standing side by side. To the logic
of this day—why we chose this moment,
this man, this side by side. The day is clear.
The photo-to-come a grainy
black and white, a flimsy square to sit
forever in guidebook fold or dusty frame.

Side by side. Our bodies match
the tilts and shadows we've felt in everything—
bus doors, a bird cage in a shop nearby,
the chocolate vender who waits for the pose
to end, who claps when the flash goes—our
moment of dazzle, even in the sun. The man
unbends from his black, rubs his hands,
fiddles, wrestles with the negative case. We wait
for the photo, say no, no chocolates now.

ABOUT THE AUTHOR

William Snyder has published poems in *Atlanta Review, Poet Lore*, and *Southern Humanities Review* among others. He was the co-winner of the 2001 Grolier Poetry Prize; winner of the 2002 Kinloch Rivers Chapbook competition; The CONSEQUENCE Prize in Poetry, 2013; the 2015 Claire Keyes Poetry Prize; and Tulip Tree Publishing *Stories That Need To Be Told* 2019 Merit Prize for Humor. He teaches writing and literature at Concordia College, Moorhead, MN.

www.ingramcontent.com/pod-product-compliance
Lightning Source LLC
Chambersburg PA
CBHW021126080526
44587CB00010B/651